Soothsayer
of the Sea

Instagram: @theRootoftheRise

Soothsayer
of the Sea

Katie Dobbs

Dedication

To Bennett:

You are my sunshine
my only sunshine who
believes in Mommy's
"cursive" and whom I
love fiercely every day

To Chris:

The philosopher's stone
didn't need to manifest the
golden friendship betwixt
alchemy and botany
for my roots flourished due
to your magic words:
I believe in you

To You:

For the inspiration
Always

To the Susan Delete Crew:

Each of you will always
hold a special place
in my heart

Choice is rooted in our lives.

It is rooted in poetry.
It is rooted in this book.

The magic* you choose to create is left up to you.

No wand required

Once upon a time...

The introduction to most fairytales and adventures that evolve around choice begin with, "Once upon a time."

For example, the choice to bite the apple, trade fins for feet, and follow a late rabbit down a hole all led to lessons learned to gain the coveted "Happily ever after."

Yet, both are subjective and aren't always happy.

I prefer to view "Once upon a time" as the creator of the "Happily ever after" magic of choice.

The magic of choice is created by choosing the path to self-revelation, whether it be the right or wrong path, there will always be an end result based upon the sum of our choices.

This book was created for you to read in the way that you choose. You have the choice to follow the traditional path by reading the pages in order. You have the choice to select the title of the path that most intrigues you and follow its lead. You will also have the choice to diverge from either path to share yourself with the world if that is where your journey takes you.

Each time you read this book; I hope you find yourself on a new journey of self-discovery. I hope you find what you are looking for. After all, our choices take us to where we are supposed to be...

Definitions and Directions

Soothsayer (n.):
a person who predicts the future by magical, intuitive, or more rational means.

Sea (n.):
a vast expanse or quantity of something.

Soothsayer of the Sea (n.):
a person who creates their own future by the unquantifiable choices they make each day

To begin, turn to the next page to continue on the straight and narrow path or choose from the fork in the road below to navigate through the book on a journey of your own making.

Near Future pg. 3 OR Sewn Unknowns pg. 14

Mingled Tears

I am the salt
saturating your skin
Replaceable
A washable sweat
surfacing to be cleansed
after whims and forgotten

She is the blood
inked into your skin
Permanent
A waterproof etching
of the home inside
the dermis of your soul

Tears mingle
with blood and dilute

Tears mingle
with salt and become

One*

* *blood, sweat, and tears*

Take Me To Church pg. 21 OR Last Rites pg. 8

Root Cause

Manipulation resides close
to Love's healthy garden
The aroma from the
flowers mistakenly hide
the stench of deception

Lies reside close
to Truth's safe haven
The sweet bliss from
kind words disguising the
bitterness of fabrication

Pain resides close
to Tenderness's comfort
The swelling of a
compassionate heart
deflated by the small
prick of a pin

Escape resides close
to Fear's unknown
The exit sign glow
leading the way
dimmed low by the
shadow of doubt

Courage resides close
to Freedom's proclamation
The prowess of spirit inherited
and strengthened by the
will to survive

Power resides close
to Wisdom's rallying cry
The declaration recited
clearly summoning those
ready to make a change

The power in change
starts at the root
The pace of the rise
is left up to you

                              The End

our future is unknown, our end ever near

Wilt With Longing pg. 22 OR Tunes of You pg. 35

Duet of Hearts

Your skin is rich
under my pale pink lips
an earthy hue under ethereal dew
fair frost pressed upon sienna dusk
northern love set in southern lust

A dichotomy of soulmates at bay
the epitome of yin and yang
yet both remain parallel parked
between the things we don't mean
and the things we don't mean to say

Mingled Tears pg. 1 OR Pores Pour pg. 57

Sea Seize

Heartsick tides flounder
under listless lullabies

Farewell* swells sway
to the call of seagulls

Salt-kissed nautilus
flow into ebbing wounds

Drowning eyes sink
in anchored goodbyes

Bon Voyage

What If pg. 29 OR Dead End pg. 63

* we were chiseled into existence by devoted artistry

Stolen Skies

I stole you from the cliff where you resigned
yourself to a life of permanent stoicism
on the edge of love yet not alive

You stole me from the cliff where I gazed
into the horizon wondering if I could fly
into the arms of love without meeting
the bottom of the sky

Our quarried sorrows heisted away
any doubt in the beauty of the love
shared on the other side of pain

Because when we are together
our stolen kisses pump life back
into our once marbled veins

Pen of Passion pg. 50 OR Botanical Courtship pg. 118

Last Rites

I am half agony, half hope
wedged between the liminal space
of limitless alternative narratives
that led the way into the weeds
only to sprout for centuries in order
to be reborn into hopeful trees
that stand witness to the agonies of
broken hearts given last rites
by the meteors of the night

Roam Wild pg. 92 OR Next Time pg. 125

Laden Shapes

The overcast sky
reminds me of your eyes

Their depths distant
heavy with resistance
bottled, contained
holding onto pain
that can only be
released when
it rains

Still, to this day,
my gaze searches
skies for shapes,
hoping to find
you in the wisps
of laden gray

Retrograde Rainbow pg. 79 OR Duet of Hearts pg. 4

Disguised Butterflies

A project unprojected
inched without a ruler
to measure the immeasurable
possibilities of the future

The checks remain unbalanced
The t's remain uncrossed
The boxes remain empty
The line in the sand lost

An imperfect specimen pinned
by a beating* heart with questions
fills in the blanks with blankets
to uncover itself with presence

Presents of knowledge that
worthiness becomes worthy
when hope sways a nonbeliever
into a balanced, crossed, full,
found dreamer

* disguised butterflies

Intimate Weaponry pg. 54 OR Stolen Skies pg. 7

Salted Wounds

you poured salt
on my wounds
but I couldn't
feel the pain
the burn is
diminished but
the decay remains
preserved, frozen,
and locked away
inside a paradigm
shift gone astray

Repose of Hope pg. 140 OR Lashes of Infinity pg. 42

Time Language

I tap my wrist
mimicking the language of time
Posing a question in pantomimes
thinking as I am seen but not heard

What is the time?
There is never enough of it yet sometimes too much of it

What is time?
A human construct to measure the timeline of a lifetime

What is?
Time stands still in the moments that matter

Sea Seize pg. 5 OR Red Pin pg. 68

what is your time language?

Sewn Unknowns

Lullaby retrospections
tuck me in bed at night
under a quilt* of questions

sewn unknowns

I feel as if we are stuck in time
waiting for the fire to reignite a world
that will never be the same; will never
heat with the same flame

What happens next?

It is a question cadenced like a
chanting lullaby as I tuck myself
into bed each night under a
questioning quilt of tomorrows

Storm Thorns pg. 99 OR Surface Level pg. 85

Errant Keys

The truth is powerful.

The gritty messy self-truths we ignore and avoid begin to manifest a skeleton key we unknowingly carry. This is the key that is accessible to each door locked tight in our minds and hearts. The secrets we tuck away in chains, the pain we hide from, the lies we live in to appease ourselves and others.

These falsehoods nurture our disillusionments and lock us out. The only door we are unlocking each day is not the one inside of ourselves. Therefore, we will continue to fumble with each errant key day after day, year after year until we find that there is not another key left on the chain of what we believed was the ring of truth.

The truth doesn't need us to carry it in the darkness of our pockets. The truth carries the power to unlock the forgiveness and tenderness we've always needed but neglected. It will free us from the shadows of shame that have followed in our wake each day. It will swing the doors open to allow the homecoming that awaits us when we decide to unlock the right door.

The truth is always there waiting to be found.
Self-discovery is where your truth resides.
You are the skeleton key.
Unlock your doors.

You are home.

Unrequited Haunts pg. 73 OR Laden Shapes pg. 9

After These Ads

Now I understand
I was only ever meant to be
the commercial entertainment
between your favorite shows
because I'm home alone while
you're cuddled up next to her
fast-forwarding through
someone you used to know
rushing to the next episode
while I remain in the break

Waiting...

Chiseled Sand pg. 111 OR If Only pg. 105

Leased Terms

Leased with terms*
the resale value of the heart
lessens after each return
for there is no warranty
left to cover the damage
inflicted

> *there are never any guarantees of happiness or
> avoiding sadness; there is only hope that we choose the
> right coverage for our hearts next time and know when
> to return it in the present when it isn't enough*

Sunshine Scars pg. 136 OR Burnt Façade pg. 129

Don't Speak

A scalding slide
of coffee scoured
my tender flesh as it
slid inside the divide

It brought to mind
all the times I held
my burning tongue

A sensation now a
memory* because
I no longer accept
nor swallow down
what burns me

** too many times, I didn't
speak up for myself
too many times, I kept silent
too many times, I was afraid
of being judged
too many times, I sacrificed my
identity for someone else's needs
too many times, I loved where
love wasn't warranted
too many times became too
many times and that is what
I have learned*

too many times is too many

Marco Polo pg. 94 OR Half Life pg. 61

*I will rise from the ashes but first I must burn

Seen Unseen

The space I hold for you that you don't catch:

In your arms watching you dream in a world I cannot reach / The pause in my breath when you say my name / A door you will never come home through / A wallet that will never hold your value / The expanse between reality and meant to be / My fingertips as they trace my name into skin they cannot claim / The song my heart sings when you smile at me / The longing after every short goodbye

Pouring Pain pg. 150 OR Time Language pg. 12

Take Me to Church

Lit through stained glass eyes
the pews curtsy, paving a path as
candled prayers dance in reverie

The breeze of loyalty sways my way
through the crossing, to faithfully rest
in the sacred silence of our love's altar

In the apse of your arm, I lay, praying
under the divine eye for a sign
that our devotion is not a sin

The sign of sanctity beats steadily
into my ear, from within his chest
I am blessed to hear my favorite hymn
His heart – Him

Unknown Light Source pg. 38 OR Two Moons pg. 78

Wilt with Longing

I text you every day but never push send
I delete, retype, and delete again
I can't – for the last foray into the
jungle of my emotions left me
without a map in a melee of rain

I can't close the door
my foot is stuck in the way
jammed between like an ellipsis*
waiting to receive a response from
a message I never sent

* ...

I love you**
we're okay
take my hand
remove your foot
I'm here to stay

*** the response never received from a message never sent*

Grime of the Gray pg. 75 OR Leased Terms pg. 17

Unglued Misdemeanors

Papier-mâché lips
modeled from ink and paper
dried quickly under exhaled
blushed hues of warm CO_2

The glossy ideals applied in
fine print were asterisked
left unread, unsaid, and
blatantly missed when kissed

A binding contract built
from tongue twisters and
relationship misdemeanors
now lay dampened, smudged,
and unglued

Heart Lines pg. 123 OR Peter Pan pg. 146

*always

Meet Me There

Lying next to you in the dark with your heartbeat in my ear;
I fall asleep unconsciously knowing you will meet me there.

There is a destination beyond, with a warm crackling
hearth, lighting the chamber where our intertwined souls
are at peace. It is the home of our connection and the
foundation of our chemistry.

Meet me there – where reality fades into the fog of
unconsciousness. There is magic there too but no wand,
potion, or spell incanted is required for admission. Entry is
granted only to the awakened magic that possesses the love
of soulmates and kindred spirits.

Meet me there – where love has no restraints,
responsibilities, or sadness. There is no darkness here, no
obstacles, no evil, just light. Light that does not blind
because love isn't blinding. Love is openness, freedom, and
unbinding. Its glow simmers tranquilly and is just enough
to light the paths we must take to reach each other in the
space between.

Meet me there – where time ceases, burdens surrender, and
the keys are accessible to release the protective chains we
have locked on our own hearts.

Meet me there – where beauty of presence is majestic and
flows like the rivers: golden and sweet. Words are not
needed when you can feel each breath and touch with
sensual otherworldly senses.

Meet me there – where golden rivers are our sheets and
your kiss my delectable dessert. We swim throughout the
night in our sweet love dreading the moment that we must
desert our endeavors and abandon them to reality.

Meet me there – where you are mine and I am yours.
Meet me there – where you let me love you.

There is not much time left as dawn approaches and the astral magic starts to whither. Hold my hand, kiss me one more time, and look into my eyes as I tell you how much you are loved.

Let's go now, together.

The sun rises as I stir awake and open my eyes to the realization that it was all just a dream. I turn to you as you groggily wake up enough to tell me goodbye with your dimpled smile and a swift kiss.

I get up to leave, I must go now, the day awaits, when I hesitate at the door…

I tiptoe back to the bed and whisper a question softly in your ear:

Meet me there? Tonight?

I lean in to hear your sleepy response and watch your lips move into a dreamy grin as they form the word:

Always

Rock Riddles pg. 86 OR Fate's Loom pg. 145

Shapeshifter

If I could shift shapes
I would fit
a square into mc
to convert our energy
into relativity

If I could shift shapes
I would mold different
forms into the same thing
so, love and light could travel
between two souls, infinitely

If I could shift shapes
I would deem that the matter
was never a theory; it was
scientifically, a proven
timeless affinity

Salted Wounds pg. 11 OR I Choose You pg. 60

A Chaotic Symphony

The clock on the wall
beats in sync with the construction outside
The nails shoot rapid-fire, orchestrating
a chaotic symphony of time passing by
as the building rise higher and higher

I stay low, dwarfed by new growth,
surrounded by stone, serenaded
by echoes reminding me to let go
of the fear of the unknown

That keeps me home watching
the world at a distance through
my kitchen window

Alone

Word Play pg. 131 OR Formal Secrets pg. 109

What If

I reach
down deep for this gift
sit here with my pen
set my mind adrift
but all I manage to pull
out are remaining
scraps of what if's

What if
I didn't mourn
what I already left behind

What if
I burned my past to ash to watch
my remembers wile away in embers

What if
your raven-colored lies flew into true
skies to become my sunny side lullabies

What if
curtains closed on the unknown
ignoring the urge of an encore keeping score

What if
I always write about you so I will
never forget how to

What if
the answers to all my questions reside
in the reflections of the restricted section

What if…
        What if…
                What if…

Atom Eyes pg. 138 OR Liminal Space pg. 46

Complex Shackles

My wrist's ached as the
burn from the words

"You're very complex"*

shackled my identity
to complexity

* Rubik's cube blues

Tunnel Vision pg. 65 OR Eye Spy pg. 44

Literary Journey

A bookmark* is like an old friend
the tassel waves in greeting
excited to join you, to be held in your hand
until it is time, to wave goodbye as it
patiently holds space for you again

> *the bookmark that holds me
> between the pages of all my
> favorite stories belongs to you*

Are We There Yet pg. 91 OR Root Cause pg. 2

*you, me, and the moon make three ~ dream family

Stars of Knight

Resting in darkness
comforted by pillowed clouds
filled with the downy of our dreams
       The Stars of Knight
guard us safely in our slumber

Galactic bound by celestial oath
to grant our wishes, give us hope,
and guide us home

Untamed Soul pg. 67 OR Errant Keys pg. 15

Hourglass Memories

The treasured sand
of our hourglass slowly
flowing into the sea
of a beloved memory
will never wash away
what once was
what should have been

After These Ads pg. 16 OR Wait pg. 100

Tunes of You

I like to imagine
that our hearts
are in tune as
I play the piano
in hopes that the
chords I choose
sound just like you
choosing me too

Resurrection pg. 113 OR Seen Unseen pg. 20

Pickled Praise

Aluminum foil praise
preserves the sweet spot until
it is unwrapped and placed
on the tongue to softly melt
into the abyss of nothingness
as if it never existed*

because it didn't

Don't Speak pg. 18 OR Human Canvas pg. 143

Shrouded Truth

They were
like the stories held dear
the books protected from the light
that carry the danger of desolation
should the truth within their shrouded
mahogany sanctuary, sheltering shelved
mysteries of misfortune, long scented
by secrets, reveal their fragile pages
too soon

Sepia Sunrise pg. 87 OR Mothership pg. 112

Unknown Light Source

FADE IN:

EXT. A LINE DRAWN IN THE SAND – UNKNOWN LIGHT SOURCE

WE OPEN on a division of past and future. The past meets the future in the present at the Equator Café of WAS and IS for a cup of steaming hot coffee, with a splash of reminiscing, and battle-scarred cookies

Memory Lane:

TEAM WAS rests in the lounge of the Dark Axis of Desertion

> TEAM WAS:
> (prepping for deception in camouflage)
>
> My house was not a home
> a funhouse bent by illusion
> My heart was not my light
> jaded in shades of corruption
> My sanctuary was robbed
> a heist of spirit and self-love
> My nature was in question
> altruistically disguised

CUT TO:

TEAM IS rests in the breeze and dances with the hopeful leaves of daydreams

> TEAM IS:
> (prepping for enlightenment in abundance)
>
> My house is a home
> it lies within my soul
> My heart is my light
> a sapient green aura
> My sanctuary is fulfilling
> decorated in boundaries
> My nature is the answer
> the survival of the fittest

JUMP TO:

TEAM IS victory over TEAM WAS

The battle that built a throne in I AM

                    I AM (V.O.):

              I am deserving
              I am acceptance
              I am love

          My broken pieces are loved
          They are whole inside of me

                              FADE OUT:

Scent Sense pg. 52 OR Sob Stories pg. 116

*the light kisses the darkness down the median of my soul

Aloof Truths

Behind my distant hills is a heart
that loves deeply but too often it finds
that the mountains want to receive all
the love and glory without giving an inch

They tend to forget that without
the hills and valleys there would
be no mountaintops

They don't see that without adequate
reciprocity there is only me and
I cannot bleed for what isn't given

I can only numb self-doubt in self-love
while they remain grandiose and alone
because once you reach the mountaintops
all that is left is the descent

Snowflake Tears pg. 147 OR Puddles of Glee pg. 135

Lashes of Infinity

I come forth with hesitance
Pay for mercy with a few pence
I place my wrists together
for him to tie above my head

His face in shadow, blinded
to conceal his emotional presence
I close my eyes in preparation
vulnerable, waiting, and anticipating

      Love

but tonight, is different

I have become his sacrifice
a gift to the night, goodbye
shades of gray area no longer
fifty for the lashes of infinity
trickle red, down my leg, in
the deathly hallowed hues of

      The End

Meet Me There pg. 25 OR Feast or Famine pg. 93

Junction of Dysfunction

Lightning flashes
powered synapses pour
Destructive thoughts align
forecasting thunderstorms
The conscious recall connects
yet it no longer transfers
The memories of us
      stranded
at the junction where
   Nobody answers

Uncertain Wounds pg. 70 OR Shapeshifter pg. 27

Diverge

Welcome to the diverge path; I'm glad you decided to join me here. This path is a pit-stop. It gives you the opportunity to collaborate on a poem with me.

I will begin, and you may choose to finish what I started.

Once complete, if you would like me to share our collaboration with the world, please tag me on Instagram @theRootoftheRise, and I will share our creation in my stories and save it to the Diverge highlight.

When you finish, or if you decide not to collaborate, then proceed with your travels on the paths offered below.

Poem Title: Eye Spy

The eye sees
what it destroys

Memory Wheel pg. 122 OR Salty Messages pg. 95

sadness dances in the dark to the melody of a broken heart

Liminal Space

I feel or does it feel me?
Lost in liminal space, outer space, air-bending
running out of oxygen, gasping for freedom
Unsure what to do with myself in this space race
between where I am and where I am supposed to be
Is it called Final Destination or just destiny?

Where am I?

Like Waldo: red, white, red, white it doesn't fit quite right
Blending into a crowd, surrounded, but invisible
to the naked eye, while I sweat in this Freddy Krueger
threaded sweater of bad dreams where bad things
come to life... 1 – 2, Freddy's – Oh shit, it's coming for you

Where am I?

Searing fingers of pain found in my nightmares
chasing, I'm running from the Jason's of my past
where 13 wasn't lucky, it almost got me
Yet I wake up once again in liminal space
An office space full of faces, turned to me for answers,
the luxury of being seen when I'd rather go back to
my bad dreams than be found where I am most Lost
The price paid here doesn't measure the out-of-pocket cost

Where am I?

Wes Craven, is that you?
Oh hell, I swerved into my brother's avenue
Scary movies, Scream dreams bring more nightmares
created by robot fiends screwing up my brain so I
drop myself off at the kiddie elixir, diving off the deep end
in order to miss this R-rated misadventure

Where am I?

Duunn, dunnn, duuuunnn, dunn…Done
drowning in this dream, where Jaws are sharp
and humans are eating my spleen, no wait, that's my heart
Bubbles of blood, turn into squelching mud, sucking
me down, laughter rings loud in my ears for I know
I will not be found under unhallowed ground

Where am I?

I'm right here, in the upside-down
where Stranger Things are not things
I'm conscious, not scared but keep running upstairs
Lips on mute, no sound comes out
until I force myself to stop, turnabout

I come face-to-face with my destiny's conception
Your serial questions knifed through the deceptions

How do you do? What's your name? Who are you?

I'm fine
My name is…
I don't know, do you?

Who am I?

Life Delights pg. 142 OR Disguised Butterflies pg. 10

Crazed Porcelain

My crazed porcelain skin
is a glazing defect

Instilled from within the kiln
the knowledge that my design is riven

Cracking from unstable tension
into a web of a thousand pieces

It crumbles until all that remains
is the dust of the unlovable

Waiting to be swept
beneath the rug and forgotten

Basking Essence pg. 74 OR Complex Shackles pg. 30

Mirrored Reflections

I look in the mirror and see:

Dreams floating in my curls / Memories fading with the hue of the blue underneath my eyes / Soft Snow White skin / Dimpled thighs that smile / Open arms that receive by letting go / Sensual lips laid over rocky steppe teeth / Prisms of optimism / Soulful shadows elusively lurking / Astral rays of hope and tender self-growth / Fingerprints left behind by a touch / A collection of life lessons / Honeyed intimacy / An unsolved mystery waiting to be recovered / Lipstick painted wishes / Reminders to make it count / Stains left by tears never wiped away / Lingering magic / A skeleton key unlocking chains of harbored pain / Volumes of Love / Manifested wisdom / The horizon of my becoming

Unglued Misdemeanors pg. 23 OR I Release You pg. 66

Pen of Passion

I wrote you a letter, guided by a pen of passion
then folded my confessions into rectangle fashion
I closed the envelope with my lips, kissed a stamp,
then added your name with my fingerprints

I don't know your address, street, avenue, or direction
so, I addressed it to 143 Fate Street, a mapped intersection

I waved goodbye, wished for a safe trip
Fingers-crossed that the journey correctly shipped

Then...

I wait, I wait, and I wait
Oh great! That means the street wasn't Fate

I pondered this catastrophe, lacerating all of my hopes
draining down, bubbling tears lathered with soap

You'll never break open what my lips sealed
nor ever know how I feel, for real

All the scenarios, kisses, and touches imagined together
were banished from my mind forever, for
in my mailbox, weeks later, I found my letter

The feeling was familiar, the disappointment typical
It read: Return to Sender – Not Deliverable

Literary Journey pg. 31 OR Flaming Ash pg. 83

Drive Safely – Operational Instructions

You are worthy of fulfilling relationships that do not require dysfunction to prosper

The compassionate love you share with yourself will open the doors of your soul to compassionately love others

Don't push people away to see if they will return

Don't revel in the validation of their return as proof that you are wanted and worthy

Don't push people away so you can be the victim when they don't show up or come back

Don't expect people to show up for you when you aren't even showing up for yourself

Don't use victimized proof to uphold the manipulated false truths you have created for yourself

Stay open to lessons of pain and heartache, love in all of its glorious capacities, thrive while living in truth, and bask in the acceptance that you are the only one in charge of your self-worth

You may be the driver, but you are also the passenger of your journey

Take care of your heart
Nurture your soul

Drive safely

Orange Sherbet Dreams pg. 80 OR Fate's Loom pg. 145

Scent Sense

His smell is like a drug to me
A hint of scent, and for a fleeting moment,
the gulls don't cry, the winds cease
sugarcoating the sand, and the moon pauses
in the sky long enough to slow the tides
as time pantomimes the moment you left
me behind with your hoodie and a bottle
with a few drops that explained everything
so clearly to one born of the salt and the sea*

The irony that the parting gift of my siren's
essence, labeled The Ocean, should return myself to me

* a Pisces

Stars of Knight pg. 33 OR Shrouded Truth pg. 37

*she, a mermaid of the sea, will always love the fisherman who caught what he couldn't keep

Intimate Weaponry

Save your story
for the people that want
to know it, intricately
to hold it, intimately
to cherish it, closely

More importantly,
save your story
from the people
that will use it as
weaponry

Secrets of Shells pg. 90 OR Pickled Praise pg. 36

Uncharted Territory

I did not see
your dandelion wisps
reaching out to me

Instead, I blew them away

I blew it
I blew it
I blew it

Until the day your text
relayed there would be no
rekindling anything between
<insert our names>

Glimpsing through the smoke
of exhaled hits of pain
I marveled at the sight,
in black and white, of our
names in print, side-by-side

Together

on the edges of the
uncharted territory of

Forever

Arms of Autumn pg. 124 OR Aloof Truths pg. 41

Edge of Concrete

The rustling wind runs its fingers
through my hair, whispers in my ear
the tale of the doe, the tortoise, and the bridge
that live in harmony upon the edge of a concrete
paradise, that too often reflects how I feel inside the
duality of synchronicity so, I leaned into the arms of
Mother Nature and believed her when she said,

"Listen, trust me"

Closed Curtains pg. 81 OR Hourglass Memories pg. 34

Pores Pour

I worked out today
I worked out today in hope
I worked out today in hope of sweating
I worked out today in hope of sweating away my thoughts

Hoping that the pores pour forth from
my skin the cooling relief I seek

Hoping that the weight from my chest
would be lifted away with each rep

Hoping that the strain on my body would
take my breath away before I could cry
out your name

Hoping that the music turned up a few
levels louder might drown out the sound
of my perforating heart

I worked out today
I worked out today in hope

Hoping that the feelings I have for you – go away

Yet, they stay

Poised Diversion pg. 133 OR Drive Safely pg. 51

Baffling Bait

Bait was cast
upon a still pond
rippling circles to the shore

Neither you nor I
knew that what was
caught that day
could ever wriggle free
from our grasp and escape

Away

Feed the Birds pg. 106 OR Fragile Feelings pg. 76

* I sail the word sea on waves of insanity with
a pen full of pain and a heart full of you

I Choose You

I've been waiting
for a loyalty that
exists amidst two
who would risk
everything they
they had to lose
to love inside the
lines in unfaltering
shades of
I choose you

Nowhere Stairs pg. 88 OR Curated Compromises pg. 132

Half Life

Half life
Half love
Half truth

My heart aches
from the halves
that keep me from
the whole I have
never been able
to attain

A Chaotic Symphony pg. 28 OR Shore Things pg. 114

Sips of Amusement

Each morning, I warm my hands
intimately on a mug of coffee
stamped with my name and sip
on the irony that it too has been
labeled without consent for
amusement

Compromised Conditions pg. 130 OR Baffling Bait pg. 58

Dead End

I don't remember the name
of the person you told me to be

I no longer rekindle those
dead end memories

Labyrinth Remnants pg. 127 OR Babes in Toyland pg. 69

* they say love is blind, but my eyes dance in your light

Tunnel Vision

My heart
is the tunnel
with the light
on the other side
waiting for you
to arrive

Enchanting Tides pg. 121 OR Home Sweet Home pg. 72

I Release You

Swinging
from your love
was such a high
that the breeze
from the drop*
brought tears
to my eyes

goodbye

Crazed Porcelain pg. 48 OR My Love is Enough pg. 104

Untamed Soul

The rainforest
of my soul
remains untamed
except for the path
I paved for you
that is clear
and full of wild
possibilities

Reigning Ringlets pg. 97 OR Blind Visionary pg. 126

Red Pin

in my dream home
there is a map, pierced
with thousands of red pins

each red mark
a curious possibility
a daydream destination
a wanderlust of desire

a pushing reminder that
the miles traveled
the seas crossed
the wonders witnessed

matter not

for I am already in my
favorite destination

Our home

Nosebleed Section pg. 107 OR Confetti Blessings pg. 84

Babes in Toyland

You crawled in
under my skin and
said I felt like home

You conquered
centuries of sentries
at the gate of my heart
and said this is my castle

You checked
underneath my bed
and said you'd protect me
from the monsters in my head

You framed
pictures of the future
on the walls of my soul
and said we would fill
them with memories

You promised
to cure my broken heart
and said you had the remedy

You
You lied
You toyed
You disguised
You

You were the boy that cried wolf
                    a phantom
                        a sheep
All the while, the only thing
I ever wanted was to follow
your heart home

If Only pg. 105 OR Mothership pg. 112

Uncertain Wounds

Release the hands
of uncertainty
that are choking
the lifeblood of
Hope
from reaching
the marrow
of your
wounded
soul

Propriety of Anxiety pg.139 OR Edge of Concrete pg. 56

*I gaze through the pane
as if a bird, perched
upon the windowsill
searching for its
inspiration to sing

Home Sweet Home

Today, I opened the door to a space that inhabits
everything I love with my heart and soul

Today, I opened the door to the wonderful
feeling of peace and comfort

Today, I opened the door and found myself
again waiting to welcome me inside

Today, when I opened my front door
for the first time in a very long time

I was home

Neither Ahead Nor Behind pg. 149 OR Root Cause pg. 2

Unrequited Haunts

Sleep evades
this restless mind

Love unrequited
haunts my sheets

Memories short
the juncture sweet

Sadness seizes
my soul
begging
you to not

Let go

Punctual Disappointment pg. 119 OR Uncharted Territory pg. 55

Basking Essence

A mountain of responsibilities
built over my calling and dreams
Lies waiting inside my soul
underneath last autumn's leaves

I hear it in the canyon of my heart,
in the echoes, I understand its cry
The ache for change resonating
in my bones, the fate, and
the reasons why

The rumble of the mountain,
the earthquake within preparing
to break open and shake loose
my doubts that are interfering

The long halted will continue
on this destined journey
The path to whom I'm meant to be
my vision no longer blurry

To choose to move on
to navigate a brand-new chapter
but most of all I yearn to inhale deep
and bask in the essence of my

Happily, Ever After

The End

Grime of the Gray

I want to stop rushing in a world that moves at an exhaustive pace. I want to laugh loudly in a quiet crowded room. I want to examine reality without rose-colored glasses. I want to love regardless of my direction. I want to write even when the ink starts to run dry. I want to explore my mind's eye and accept what I see. I want to acknowledge what isn't said and speak the truth. I want to dream without nightmares and rest in my favorite spot. I want to read, travel, and escape but still remain present. I want to feel cruel words die before they reach my heart. I want to honor my mess-ups, failures, and losses but still admire the covert self-growth under the grime of the gray. I want most of all to see beyond what is tirelessly fed, shift fear into curiosity, lean further into change, and welcome whatever comes forth with grace and integrity.

Next Time pg. 125 OR Sunshine Scars pg. 136

Fragile Feelings

I am tired
of loving fragile
hearts that do not
pump life back into me

Instead, I love so fiercely
they shatter in my hands
leaving scars that never bleed

Mirrored Reflections pg. 49 OR Old Cobblestones pg. 110

*I am so I shall be

Two Moons

The lone wolf howls
at the two moons that orbit
inside of my brain

Beckoning for a pack of facts
to find their way back
from memory lane

Joining as one to prey
upon thoughts that control
the swell of the waves

Filling my eyes with their
lost cries as their misdeeds
stream down my face

Echoes & Mementos pg. 117 OR Junction of Dysfunction pg. 43

Retrograde Rainbow

The love I seek dwells
in the treasure trove
that only exists on the
other side of a renegade
retrograde rainbow

Worthless Confinement pg. 137 OR Price Tag of Excuses pg. 98

Orange Sherbet Dreams

Lilac skies blanket
orange sherbet dreams
under a canopy of a
star-crossed lover's
jet streams*

happy trails

Sips of Amusement pg. 62 OR Are You Afraid of the Dark pg. 144

Closed Curtains

The curtains closed
on an ovation
of masterful
self-preservation
when I no longer
had to pretend that
the show must go on

Pickled Praise pg. 36 OR Edge of Concrete pg. 56

*you were the sun; I was the rain
we both dissipated in the
rays of yesterdays*

Diverge

Welcome to the diverge path; I'm glad you decided to join me here. This path is a pit-stop. It gives you the opportunity to collaborate on a poem with me.

I will begin, and you may choose to finish what I started.

Once complete, if you would like me to share our collaboration with the world, please tag me on Instagram @theRootoftheRise, and I will share our creation in my stories and save it to the Diverge highlight.

When you finish, or if you decide not to collaborate, then proceed with your travels on the paths offered below.

Poem Title: Flaming Ash

Incandescent desire
fueled our fire
leaving ash
where there
was once a
flame

Sob Stories pg. 116 OR Shapeshifter pg. 27

Confetti Blessings

Yellow confetti blessings
shower from limb balconies
to ease the pain when fall leaves
by celebrating the love soon to be
found in the season of new beginnings

Dead End pg. 63 OR Word Play pg. 131

Surface Level

There are plenty of fish in the sea
kissing the surface, endlessly
searching to feed on any
nourishment without
an undercurrent

Human Canvas pg. 143 OR Word Play pg. 131

Rock Riddles

The wild
rain caught between
the riddles of the rocks and
the soothing stanzas of the stream
babble to the wind the tales of love
that steadily endure and have no end

Peter Pan pg. 146 OR Pen of Passion pg. 50

Sepia Sunrise

May the colorful
kaleidoscopic hue
of a twilight sky
inspire you to
overcome every
unexpected
sepia sunrise

Red Pin pg. 68 OR My Love is Enough pg. 104

Nowhere Stairs

I am the mansion built upon a dysfunctional plot to confuse the ghosts that haunt my foundation. The relationships that reside inside live in rooms of their own creation. However, I am the mastermind that fills each addition with doors and stairs that lead to nowhere except empty chairs that rest as decoys to entice idleness as the windows gaze upon the pain that builds and builds, trying to escape away to open space. Yet, the stays of my brain hold me tightly in place where I was designed and created to feel safe.

Fragile Feelings pg. 76 OR Pores Pour pg. 57

*excess is decadence dressed up as power

Secrets of Shells

Where do we go when we die?

Some say heaven; some say hell
Some say we are already dead
living lives of lies inside of shells

Botanical Courtship pg. 118 OR What If pg. 29

Are We There Yet

I smiled into your heartbeat
whilst I laid in your arms
The darkness hid my grin
as I was once again
lulled by your hymn
into oblivion to dream
in the melody of revelation

That a smile takes more muscles to form
than it does to shape the word goodbye

I smiled because it brought tears to my eyes
a candied tearjerker flavored in joyful sorrow

I smiled because it ticked in tune to the clock
a make it count reminder to meet me there

I smiled because it is the birthplace of us
a muscle memory of first-steps and are we there yet's

I smiled because it is the sound of my safe haven
a cloud protected by the gods of Mt. Olympus

I smiled because I knew I would never forget
the sound of you, even though you want me to

Liminal Space pg. 46 OR Atom Eyes pg. 138

Roam Wild

Let's catch our feelings
and gently nurture them
until they can be released
back into the wild to roam

free

in a love without restraints

Memory Wheel pg. 122 OR Two Moons pg. 78

Feast or Famine

Famine of spirit
Sown by cultivation
Fertilized by refuse
Tilled by rejection

Harvested* in the
season of my
transformation

a fruitful yielding

Meet Me There pg. 25 OR Curated Compromises pg. 132

Marco Polo

I was lost
fading away
losing myself
in the resting place
of other peoples
mistakes

Home Sweet Home pg. 72 OR Feed the Birds pg. 106

Salty Messages

Throw me to the sea where the salt
rubs all of my memories away

Let the waves wash clean
the grime that clings to
my shapely figure

Send me to my haven to be
welcomed by the treasures
of the mysterious deep

Rock me gently atop the waves
of my emotions that carry such
weight yet are so soft at the core

Anchor me when I begin to drift
outside the harbor, steadily
in need to be reeled back in

Warm me when my chills
need sunshine from the rain
and shelter from the cold

Find me when I am lost
my inner message spoiling
and spinning without direction

Read the message in the bottle
I threw it to find you

It reads: I need you

Pouring Pain pg. 150 OR I Release You pg. 66

*scribed end of beginnings the tale foretold
beware my dear, destiny is manifold*

Reigning Ringlets

My head of curls
a faceted crown of brown
Reigned and adorned
since the day I was born
Until one fine day, when
the war came to play

Reigning ringlets seized,
a coup d'état, lifeless corpses
of curls lay piled at my feet
Guillotined, separated from me,
like the tears that dropped
from my cheeks

A heist that stole from my soul
an identity, all I had ever known
Dethroned by a fascist invader,
dictated by a disease, a betrayer
Besieged with power to end life
a simple 'off with her head' if one
didn't fight the battle right

Although an imposter rules now
over a court of curls that belong
to the past, ghosts of a used to be
I endeavor to keep in mind that
once, long ago, purple was only
worn by royalty

A crowned color has always been
my favorite shade, ironically
Long before an autoimmune malady
ever committed treason against
my nobility

Half Life pg. 61 OR Tunes of You pg. 35

Price Tag of Excuses

You told me your affections
came with a price
A tag of taxes and fines
auto-withdrawal dues
I paid the daily fee
because I liked you

Now many months later
my pockets are empty
I can no longer pay to cater
to needs I serve as your waiter

My cup, empty, needs refilling
my feelings now up for bidding
A price not too step, an affordable
one-time sale only lies behind
on a table, solely

A purchase of choice declined
by a customer who carries cash mostly
In the second side pocket where I reside
wrapped in a wad of endlessly lonely
clipped together by

Excuses

Unknown Light Source pg. 38 OR Take Me to Church pg. 21

Storm Thorns

My self-worth muddled, my soul forlorn
you arrived as if birthed from a storm
You held my hand, loved my thorns
revived a life that was falsely adorned

Now enlightened, vividly shown
the love in trust, the magic of my own
My heart opened; you broke through
scenic secrets that no one knew

In a declaration of gratitude
the garden of my heart bloomed
Blessing my life with a view
that would always remind me of you

Errant Keys pg. 15 OR Last Rites pg. 8

Wait

A few words heard, the infection spread
a virus of term germs cemented in our heads

Pretty Princess
Powder Puff
Piece of Ass

They think we like this stuff so
they can pretend they are here to rescue us

Giving verbal presents like treats:

You're too sweet, too emotional, too bold
You're not strong enough, baby
I got you, are you cold?

Wait

Those gifts do nothing for me
I can be a princess and still slay thee
A prince is not a prince until he
earns the respect of his principality

To conquer pain, they can't always see,
being the victor doesn't equate to being tough
or being in touch with your masculinity

Yet, I regret, there's more to explore
this world isn't so clear to me anymore

Wait

Pain is the power to the one
inflicting a receiving end pass
Catching trauma on the fifty-yard lines
blurry, because booze is never choosey to the
one who was stained when lines were crossed

A score made after a splash in a glass
"Will it bother you in 10 years?" he asked
"I don't know," said a 17-year-old's tears
as she spoke her truth that fell on deaf ears

So many times, I have replayed what
I should have told him that day
I'd love to go back in time – warp his mind
I'd ask him a question this time:
"Would you say that to a daughter of your design?"
I dare not say; she may be where I am today

Wait

The criminal, the perpetrator, the player
undercover thanks to a coward he called brother
Little did you know what you would create
by ignoring my whistle blow, just wait

Granted keys to a cell, he can be reached easily
dial 911 – who you gonna call when a
buster isn't a ghost but carries a badge and
has the authority to arrest your ass-k no questions
for he will tell you lies when it probably hasn't
ever replayed in his mind

When 20 years later my answer in 10 years
wouldn't have accepted that kind of direction from
a weak man who didn't want blood on his hands

Wait

Stop the lie detector; let's play a game
Me first! Do you even remember my name?

It's the name next to the X where the buried
treasure was picked over by carrion buzzards
like you so righteous, grandiose, and shady in blue

Wait

I get another turn, see
The dice says skip the next player
that's definitely not me
I'm the dealer of questions now

Do your hands ever get sweaty when you bow?

When you smile on the TV
and pretend to save the day

Do you think I don't see you looking for your next prey?

You see, there is a sentencing for
falsifying evidence that never turns a cold ear
It's called karma, she's a clingy bitch, I hear

Similar to the ankle bracelet you should've had to wear
that feels so tight as you crouch down to prepare
by praying to yourself that you hope it isn't

Judgement Day

Quivering, for you know Hell is the only way
because your truth will never set you free

When the time comes, when the shots ring near
it will flash before your eyes all too clear
That destiny may have pulled the trigger
but it was loaded by a forgotten name:

Fear

Mirrored Reflections pg. 49 OR Rock Riddles pg. 86

* If the eyes are the window to the soul,
then why are your curtains closed?

My Love is Enough

I loved the movie
Casper as a kid
When he asks her,
"Can I keep you?"
just like you did to me
Except he stayed and
you faded away,
Slowly

Your touch became lighter and lighter
Your voice seemed to drift away
I couldn't see you when I summoned you
for you went back to the light they say

Where is the light?
What does that mean?
Does it mean greener pastures?
People and places better than me?

Loving you was my favorite fantasy
but for you I was just a human being
that distracted you from unearthly things

Maybe someday I will find the light
and you will be there waiting for me
or maybe, just maybe I won't follow
you at all and I will find love in
the mundane* things

I will find that my love is enough for me

Roam Wild pg. 92 OR After These Ads pg. 16

If Only

If only you'd set me free
I might be able to breathe

If only you'd set me free
I'd fill my lungs with relief
slowly release you from my being
exhale the toxicity that is suffocating* me

If only you'd set me free
I'd stop smothering who I am
meant to be

love lets you breathe

Basking Essence pg. 74 OR Sewn Unknowns pg. 14

Feed the Birds

I am like a carrier pigeon

Carrying messages I cannot read
Sharing advice as the crow flies
Passing words of love and wisdom

To all except the one doing the work

Duet of Hearts pg. 4 OR Life Delights pg. 142

Nosebleed Section

It tastes iron rich as
it dresses my upper lip
like a sultry red lipstick
its thick consistency
reminds me that my
blood is thicker than
the water I use to wipe
away the sins that live
beneath my skin that
pump to the surface
every now and then
so I can taste the pain
that I choke down
inside every

"I'm okay"

I Choose You pg. 60 OR Resurrection pg. 113

*I use the shadows of night to shade my skin
from the burning desires held secret within*

Formal Secrets

My closet is the width of a coffin
it holds the skeletons I clothe
in formal skirts and tuxedoes
I prepare them to be exhumed
so I may formally introduce
them to my demons

My demons roam wild
aching to be set free into
a world where people
must see to believe that
not all tales are fabled
but held close inside
hidden from the label
of wrong and right

So, until the day I am
ready for them to meet
I will continue to slip
into my coffin to greet
the secrets I keep

Salted Wounds pg. 11 OR Puddles of Glee pg. 135

Old Cobblestones

A centuries old road
paved the way with
cobblestones to teach
a wandering soul
that a path does not
have to be smooth to
lead you in the right
        direction

Drive Safely pg. 51 OR Surface Level pg. 85

Chiseled Sand

As I watch
the sands of time
slowly chisel fine lines
around my eyes

I can see that time
is kept by gravity
for they are both
grounding yet free

Inching forward
while falling quickly
until there is no
time left to keep

For one day, I will
become the sand,
and someone else
will watch me

Laden Shapes pg. 9 OR Grime of the Gray pg. 75

Mothership

Have you ever looked at the stars
and wondered which one was your mother?

Is she the North Star guiding you home?
Is she part of Orion's Belt teaching you a lesson?
Is she the Sun encouraging your growth?

She is universally nameless yet collectively
known to be the origin of light

Your mother is the star that gave you the galaxy from
her womb so you could hang your dreams on the moon

For like the stars, one day she will be gone,
but for lightyears her love will linger on

Wait pg. 100 OR Seen Unseen pg. 20

Resurrection

You can't place
a once broken girl
upon a pedestal
and not expect her to
display her imperfections
for they are where
she was restored* and
brought back to life

womanhood

Propriety of Anxiety pg. 139 OR Lashes of Infinity pg. 42

Shore Things

You told me you've never
seen snow or felt the weather get cold
as I floated on my back next to your boat

I watched your reaction
to my surprised expression,
catching the rays from your laughter
to warm my skin, relishing every morsel
of fresh pineapple you shared while
talking about our nameless dreams

To this day, I don't even know your name
or if you'd even remember me but for
a short moment in time it was just two
strangers bound by opposite longings

One for a kiss from the cold
in a land they will never see
while the other dreamed to never
leave the sea where strangers meet
near the jungle by the shore that sings
about the importance of little things

Sea Seize pg. 5 OR Leased Terms pg. 17

the call for change whispers to the wind
not all that is lost should be found again

Sob Stories

Every love story
on every screen
shakes my entire being

My molten core, burns
wanting so much more
than to be a surface
cracked open only
for pleasure

My sobs release
the pressure
I used to hold
myself together

Plates of friction
inflame my heart's
affliction

I cannot withtake
the magnitude of
another sob shaking
earthquake of
heartbreak

Intimate Weaponry pg. 54 OR Marco Polo pg. 94

Echoes and Mementos

Scents

                  linger

fragrant echoes
a heart notes
and

                  remembers

Hourglass Memories pg. 34 OR Untamed Soul pg. 67

Botanical Courtship

Love was planted
the seeds were sown
The sprouts became stems
slowly on their own
Buds became blooms
warmed by the sun
Drenched by the rain
stretched open to become
Adorned with starlight
glistening adieu
Fragrantly heady
petaled flowers anew
Tenderly nourished
my love for you grew
A botanical courtship
blessed by the
Man in the Moon

Nosebleed Section pg. 107 OR Complex Shackles pg. 30

Punctual Disappointment

I filed for
disappointment
the day the point
disappeared*

an alienation of punctuation

Storm Thorns pg. 99 OR Arms of Autumn pg. 124

*I look at each moon, hoping to see you
reflected there, looking for me too

Enchanting Tides

The waves of a translucent sea
will never be as iridescently enchanting
as the moon tide that glistens in her eyes
when she thinks of him

Crazed Porcelain pg. 48 OR Closed Curtains pg. 81

Memory Lane

A radio plays our memories
reminders selected by a host
to play host to long lost feelings
I reach for you but keep steering
because the road ahead is quiet
and dead as my empty hand
So I keep singing, out of tune,
a soliloquy to the moon because
a man once lived within her too
I drive and think, hitting speed
bumps without the brakes
because I can't stop once I start
I can't start once I stop either so
I'm stuck in the mud of my own
grudges with spinning wheels,
lost ideals, and wishes on fallen
stars that I could be in your arms
but the rearview reminds me that
I can't reach I love you without
reverse so I turn up the music
and let my tears blur the mirror

Old Cobblestones pg. 110 OR Sepia Sunrise pg. 87

Heart Lines

Don't leave your heart on

Read

by someone that can't read
the worth between your lines

Shrouded Truth pg. 37 OR Secrets of Shells pg. 90

Arms of Autumn

She ran into the arms of autumn
to be held until the frozen kiss of winter
soothed the burns that summer wrought
from the broken promises of a love affair
that scorched May's blooming heart

Chiseled Sand pg. 111 OR Salty Messages pg. 95

Next Time

The babbling brook whispers
sweet nothings to the breeze

The two pulled by the unseen
to meet again inevitably

Until a breath of wind immersed
your hand into mind so the soddened
butterflies fluttering inside could
migrate from the rocky bottom of my
rippling heart to the lifesaving breath
upon lips* that dried and revived their
wings to fly once more where
the wild things thrive

kiss me next time

Are We There Yet pg. 91 OR Literary Journey pg. 31

Blind Visionary

In this head space
it is hard to see anything

Yet there is no need to explain
to a visionary who can no longer see

That the missing piece is found
in the clarity of humility

Because eclipsed tears create
the necessary blurry reality

To explain everything clearly
unseen and untamed in

Shrouded Pain

Disguised Butterflies pg. 10 OR Confetti Blessings pg. 84

Labyrinth Remnants

I am lost

I wander in afterthoughts,
uninspired droughts, and anxiety onslaughts
searching for a remedy that doesn't exhaust

I am lost

My pen, fills with lidocaine ink
numbing each letter so I cannot feel
the piercing pain of passion that once
brought life back from death

I am lost

I marvel at the traces of nostalgia spread across
the page waiting for recognition in ceaseless incompletion
calling to me as I avoid eye contact and walk away

I am lost

Waiting to be found amongst the evidence so I can be
tagged, body-bagged, and a cold case assigned to my name
until I have been unbound from my labyrinth of disdain

I am lost

Yet I remain

Shore Things pg. 114 OR Feast or Famine pg. 93

* I can't choose us until I choose myself

Burnt Façade

Our personal stories make us who we are, yet we often hide behind reflective glass to shield ourselves from judgement.

When was the last time someone asked you the question, "What is your story?" that wasn't sarcastic or just an opening made to tell their own? When was the last time someone was truly interested in the ink you've spilled while writing all that your pages entail?

My answer, I presume, is similar to yours: a long time or maybe not ever. We continue to pass out crumbs of ourselves to others but most likely never invite anyone in to feast on our whole truth.

Turn on the stove. Burn your façade.

Fearlessly, open the door to your identity, watch the air of a half-life flood out of your heart and sweep out the crumbs left behind by the ash of who you never were.

Wilt With Longing pg. 22 OR Mingled Tears pg. 1

Compromised Conditions

There is wisdom* lingering
in the darkness between cracks
attempting to compromise
ingrained beliefs that no longer
support a foundation originally
built under precarious conditions

> *as children, we are raised on the
> foundations and beliefs of our guardians
> it is not until we begin to separately
> construct our own lives that we truly
> begin to lay the concrete of our own
> becoming

Aloof Truths pg. 41 OR Reigning Ringlets pg. 97

Word Play

Intimate word play
is my desired foreplay
I savor the climactic
vowels as they slowly
shape around the

curves

of my name
in your mouth

Repose of Hope pg. 140 OR Don't Speak pg. 18

Curated Compromises

landestine meetings
oncealed hearts
overt kisses
urated after dark

* a curtained courtship

Stars of Knight pg. 33 OR Unglued Misdemeanors pg. 23

Poised Diversion

Poised innuendos* whisper
tales of obscene scenes
layering textured gestures
upon the ruse of a prim
propriety quietly pining
for an excursion of diversion

J'ai envie de toi

Enchanting Tides pg. 121 OR Retrograde Rainbow pg. 79

I picked every petal*wishing for your love
but all I was left with was me

he loves me; he loves me not

Puddles of Glee

My old umbrella
drenched in depression
soaked in sorrow now
lays useless, abandoned

Replaced by new rainboots
to jump with liberating glee in
the puddles of all my old tears

Time Language pg. 12 OR Babes in Toyland pg. 69

Sunshine Scars

My sunshine scars
shine white in the light
to remind me that there
is divinity to behold in skin
that has lived life and given it

Tunnel Vision pg. 65 OR Neither Ahead Nor Behind pg. 149

Worthless Confinement

The extent of my worthiness
would never again be confined
to a love that wasn't my own

Uncertain Wounds pg. 70 OR Scent Sense pg. 52

Atom Eyes

The atoms of my eyes
were formed in the core
where a mere speck of
consciousness met at the
ending of the beginning

My cosmic thoughts
now reflect upon the
philosophical concept
that we were born
from the same galactic
storm to meet here
after billions of years
under the same stars
from whence we
were formed

Nowhere Stairs pg. 88 OR A Chaotic Symphony pg. 28

Propriety of Anxiety

Anxiety
fully recharged
fills my lungs with
suffocating disquiet
until it reaches the
brim once again

Deadened,
it breaks free
effortlessly spilling
over as water falls
down my cheeks

Salt
doesn't burn
on the wounds
released for their
absolution brings
me peace

Burnt Façade pg. 129 OR Stolen Skies pg. 7

Repose of Hope

My soul yearns for the repose
of an enlightened lover that
challenges me with discovery
while holding my hand in hope

Blind Visionary pg. 126 OR Echoes & Mementos pg. 117

*a rebirth of empathy lies within the depths of trauma

Life Delights

The joy
I find
in small
delights
is where
I find
myself
living
my best
life

Baffling Bait pg. 58 OR Labyrinth Remnants pg. 127

Human Canvas

You told me I deserved it
as you burned curses
into my skin

Painting upon the flesh
of a human canvas seems
farfetched until it's the skin
you're living in

Each vex creates a complex
until all that is left
is the artist's sketch

While the original masterpiece
remains hidden in plain sight
detectable only by blacklight

Punctual Disappointment pg. 119 OR Orange Sherbet Dreams pg.80

Diverge

Welcome to the diverge path; I'm glad you decided to join me here. This path is a pit-stop. It gives you the opportunity to collaborate on a poem with me.

I will begin, and you may choose to finish what I started.

Once complete, if you would like me to share our collaboration with the world, please tag me on Instagram @theRootoftheRise, and I will share our creation in my stories and save it to the Diverge highlight.

When you finish, or if you decide not to collaborate, then proceed with your travels on the paths offered below.

Poem Title: Are You Afraid of the Dark?

You'll never see me
in the dark unless I
turn on the light to
let you in

Formal Secrets pg. 109 OR Compromised Conditions pg. 130

Fate's Loom

paths
intertwine
crafted upon
fate's loom
threaded, dyed,
sunshine dried
sewed lovers
intimately
bloomed

Price Tag of Excuses pg. 98 OR Unrequited Haunts pg. 73

Peter Pan

they were
lost boys*
looking for
a found girl
to find them

looking for me
to find them
to use her
to use me
to set them free

without knowing I
have never had
will never have
the key they need

*I cannot be your crutch between
reality and who you want to be
I can only be me and the key
you seek isn't in my keeping*

Sips of Amusement pg. 62 OR Worthless Confinement pg. 137

Snowflake Tears

My tears fell softly
as I watched you go
Each a graceful snowflake
burdened by the cold

Uncharted Territory pg. 55 OR Junction of Dysfunction pg. 43

*you consume my thoughts, dreams,
and all the little à la carte things

Neither Ahead nor Behind

Do not race ahead
for I will be left behind

Do not lag behind
for I will never leave you

Poised Diversion pg. 133 OR Eye Spy pg. 44

Pouring Pain

I want to
pour my
heart out
to you
but
instead
I pour
the pain
into me

Snowflake Tears pg. 147 OR Near Future pg. 3

About the Author

Katharine was the student of the month in fourth grade: she listed her favorite subject as "Spelling" and her something special as "I like to read." Known by her friends as Katie, she resides in Oklahoma, where she is a businesswoman by day and a Mommy to a little boy at night (aka every minute of every day).

Her poetry is motivated by love, self-growth, hope, deep feeling, loss, and the perseverance of those that face a resistant path on their self-journey to rise.

She continues to enjoy her fourth grade past times but also finds pleasure in history, genealogy, collecting antique Wedgwood, laughing at Dad jokes, and daydreaming of life as a professional poet.

Her passion for "Spelling" can be found on Instagram @theRootoftheRise.

Printed in Great Britain
by Amazon

61807706R00092